Dedicated To:
Alli, Sam & Family

Written By: Abigail Gartland

Hello, my name is St. Monica!

I was born in the year 333! Can you believe that?

I had a very full life and was the mom of three children.

My daughter, Perpetua, grew up to be a religious sister!

My son, Navigius, grew up to be a priest!

My other son, Augustine, made some bad choices in his life

He became very mean, and had to leave our home.

This made me very sad. I didn't even want to show my face.

One night, I recieved a visit from our mother, Mary.

She told me to go fin my son, Augustine, and reconnect with him.

I traveled to many places, and finally found him in Milan.

By the time I found him, he was all grown up!

Augustine started making much better choices, and after a few more years, he was baptized!

I did not get to see Augustine grow into holy man during my life on earth, but I sa— it from Heaven.

am the patron saint of wives and moms!

You can celebrate m life with me on August 27th every year!

love you, and I pray for you every day of your life.

St. Monica Pray for us!

yright:

rt: © PentoolPixie © LimeandKiwiDesigns
sed purchased: 1/10/2024

About the Author

Abigail Gartland

I love the saints and I love my faith. The idea for sharing the stories of the saints with little ones came when my dear frien[d] were expecting their first baby. I wanted [to] create something as unique and special a[s] our friendship. Each book is dedicated to very special people and groups who have enriched my faith in different ways. I am blessed to write these stories and appreciate the unending support of my family and friends. When I am not writing [I] am a middle school teacher. I hope you enjoy these stories. I pray for each and every person who opens one of my books to learn more about the saints.

Abbie

www.ingramcontent.com/pod-product-compliance
Lightning Source LLC
LaVergne TN
LVHW052046070526
838201LV00087B/4903

ISBN 979-8-8692-8318-4

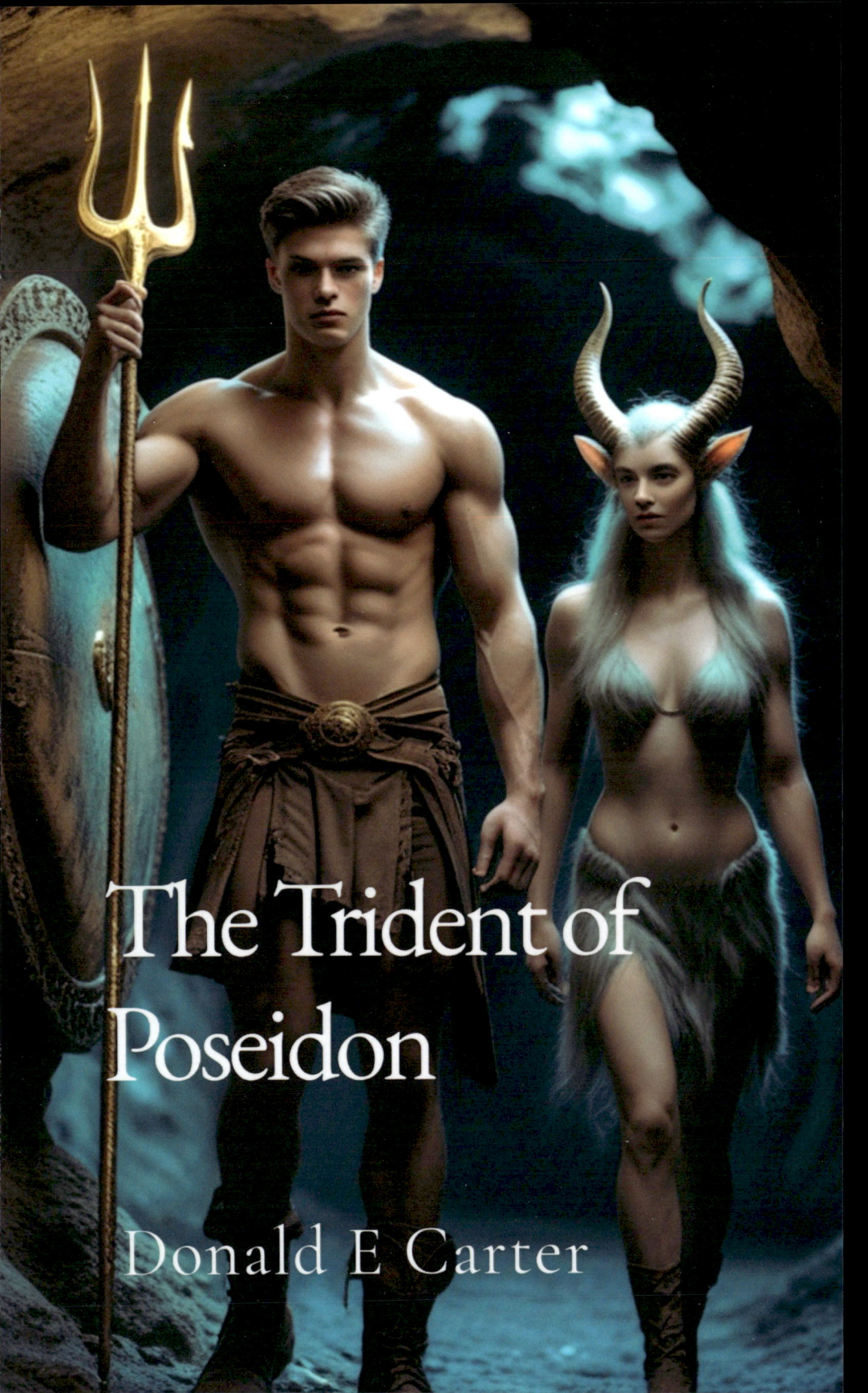